Beginning Comprehension

Contents

© Key Curriculum Publications

Acknowledgements

© Key Curriculum Publications Ltd., 1998 under licence from Evan-Moor Corporation, USA.
This material has been adapted and reproduced under licence from Evan-Moor Corporation, USA. All rights reserved. The copyright
of all materials in this book remains the property of the publisher. This edition is published by arrangement with Evan-Moor and is
adapted from a work © 1995 Evan-Moor Corporation.
No part of this publication may be reproduced or transmitted by photocopier of any other means, except pages marked 'copiable page'
which can be photocopied for use within the purchasing institution only.

The only copies that may be made without reference to the publisher are those pages marked 'COPIABLE' providing that they are for
the sole use of the students taught by the person or school buying the publication. Copies may not be made available to other schools
or individuals. Copies may not be used to form all or any part of any other publication.

All requests for reproduction and other rights must be sent in writing to:
Key Curriculum Publications Ltd., P.O. Box 293, Hemel Hempstead, HP2 7WD
e-mail: keycurric@aol.com

ISBN 1-90236-120-2

When you read a sentence, a picture forms in your mind.

Circle the sentence that matches each picture.

Mario delivered pizza
all afternoon.

Mario delivered newspapers
all afternoon.

Grandpa rested in the chair,
while Dad stood next to it.

Dad rested in the chair, while
Grandpa stood next to it.

While Tom was reading,
his puppy was playing.

While Tom was reading,
his puppy was sleeping.

Pets at School

"Get up, Ann," said Kim.
"We can take pets to school.
I do not want to be late."

"I have pet mice," said Bob.
"I give them seeds.
It is fun to have mice for pets."

"This is my pet cat," said Kim.
"He likes to sleep on my bed.
It is fun to have a cat for a pet."

"This is my dog, Mike," said Lee.
"Sit, Mike. Shake my hand.
It is fun to have a dog for a pet."

"I do not have a pet," said Tom.
"I will ask Dad if I can get a pet too."

Teacher: After reading the story complete task on page 5.

Name: _____

Read the story on page 4,
and match the answers to the
questions.

Who did Kim tell to get up?   Tom

What can the children take to school?   Ann

Who did not have a pet?   sit up

What can Lee's pet do?   pets

Who has pet mice?   cat

What is Kim's pet?   Bob

Write about your pet:

_____

_____

_____

Draw your pets on the other side.

5

Teacher: Draw a line to correct answer.

The Birthday Pet

Joey had always wanted a pet. His parents promised to get him one for his birthday. Joey wasn't sure what kind of pet he wanted. He knew it had to be small because his family live in a caravan.

On his birthday, Joey's dad took him to the pet shop to choose a pet. There were so many animals. Joey saw fish, dogs, cats, hamsters, and many more.

"It will be hard to choose," thought Joey.

Joey was staring into a fish tank when he heard a whistle and a chirp. He turned around and saw the shop keeper was holding a blue-green bird on his finger.

"This is Pete. He is a parakeet," said the shop keeper. "Would you like to hold him?"

Joey held out his finger and Pete jumped on to it. Pete walked up Joey's arm and perched on his shoulder. Joey made up his mind right then.

"This is the pet I want," said Joey. "I'll start teaching him to talk as soon as I get him home."

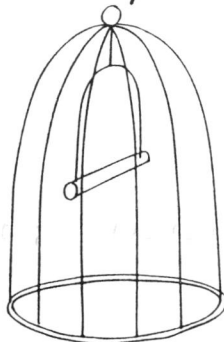

Teacher: Read story to children.

The Birthday Pet

Listen to the story.
Answer the questions.

1. Where did Joey and his family live?

2. Why did Joey's father take him to the pet shop on his birthday?

3. What kind of bird was Pete?

4. What colour was Pete?

5. Why do you think Joey picked Pete as his pet?

6. What was Joey going to teach Pete to do?

7. What do you call a person who sells you things in a shop?

8. What kind of pet would you like to have?

The Birthday Pet

Listen to the story.
Put the story in order.

Teacher: Teaching how to sequence a story.
Children to cut apart and put in correct order.

Read and Think

This story is all mixed up!
Read the sentences. Think about what is happening.
Number this story in the order it could happen.

At the Beach

_____ "But first you have to eat a good lunch."

_____ After lunch Mother took the children to the beach.

_____ "What would you like to do today?"
asked Lucille's mother.

_____ "Yes, the beach will be lots of fun!" said her
brother Thomas.

_____ "O.K. we can go to the beach," said Mother.

___1___ It was a beautiful sunny morning.

_____ The children found shells and seaweed.

_____ At sunset the children said, "Let's come back
another day."

_____ "Let's go to the beach," said Lucille.

Read and Think

It is important to understand **who** is doing things in a story.
It is also important to understand **what** is happening.
Read this story and answer the **who** and **what** questions on page 11.

Minkey the Monkey

Maria had a very interesting job. She didn't do her job alone. She had a helper named Minkey. Minkey was a monkey.

Every morning Maria and Minkey would go to the park. Maria would play lively music on her banjo while Minkey danced. People would gather around, laughing and clapping. After his dance, Minkey would hold out his hat and chatter until money was dropped into the hat.

After each show, Minkey and Maria would sit down on a park bench and share some fruit and cheese. Minkey's favourite treat was grapes. Later Minkey would take a nap in the sun.

After several shows in the park, Maria and Minkey would leave for home. The tired little monkey would ride on Maria's shoulder.

Answer these **who** questions about *Minkey the Monkey.*

1. Who helped Maria in her job?

_____

2. Who liked to take a nap in the sun?

_____

3. Who played music on a banjo?

_____

4. Who sat on the bench and ate fruit and cheese?

_____

• •

Answer these **what** questions about *Minkey the Monkey.*

1. What was Maria's job?

_____

2. What was Minkey's job?

_____

3. What did people do when Minkey held out his hat and chattered?

_____

It is important to understand **when** things happen in a story.
Read this story. Then answer the questions on page 13.

A Stormy Week

The weather in the first week of January was awful! Every day there was another storm! It seemed as if all of the storms for the year were coming in one week.

The wind blew all day on Sunday and it was very cold. By afternoon the wind was so strong that it blew down the clothes line in the garden. When he had finished watching the football match my father went out to put it up again.

The next day it rained very hard, and my feet were soaking wet by the time I got to school. My teacher helped me put the wet shoes and socks in a warm, dry place. By 10:00 my feet were warm, and my shoes and socks were dry.

During the night, the rain turned to snow. When we woke up on Tuesday morning, the ground was covered with snow. We could not go to school, but we could make snowmen and snow angels in the garden. School was still closed on Wednesday.

We went back to school on Thursday. Some of the snow had melted in the warm morning sun. By afternoon it turned cold again. The melting snow turned to ice on the pavements and playground. The ice was too slippery to play on, so we had to stay inside. Perhaps Friday would be warm and sunny. That would make it the best day of the week!

Answer these **when** questions about *A Stormy Week.*

1. When did we make snowmen and snow angels?

   _____

2. On which days was school closed?

   _____

3. By what time did my feet feel warm and dry?

   _____

4. When did the wind blow down the clothesline?

   _____

5. When was my father watching football?

   _____

6. In which month was it very stormy?

   _____

Draw a snowy, windy day.

┌───┐
│   │
│   │
│   │
│   │
│   │
│   │
│   │
└───┘

Hide and Seek

John invited all his friends to come to the park on Saturday for a game of hide and seek. Everyone liked to play this game at the park because there were many good places to hide.

Sam climbed a big tree and sat very still on a wide branch. When Sally tried to find him, she walked right past the tree, but she didn't see Sam.

Mary saw a good place to hide by the picnic tables. She crawled into a cave made by some low bushes. She sat very still and was as quiet as a mouse. Gary looked, but he never found the cave.

Danny slid under a bench behind the playing field. He could see Tom looking for him, but he was so still even his shadow didn't move!

When it was time to go home, the friends all thanked John for inviting them to play. They all had a good time at the park.

Answer these **where** questions about *Hide and Seek.*

1. Where did Mary hide?

   _____

2. Where did Sam sit?

   _____

3. Where did John invite his friends to play?

   _____

4. Where did Danny slide?

   _____

5. Where did Sally walk?

   _____

6. Where did Gary look?

   _____

Show where you would hide at the park.

> The **main character** is the person or animal that the story is mostly about. Sometimes a story will have more than one main character.

Anita's Ants

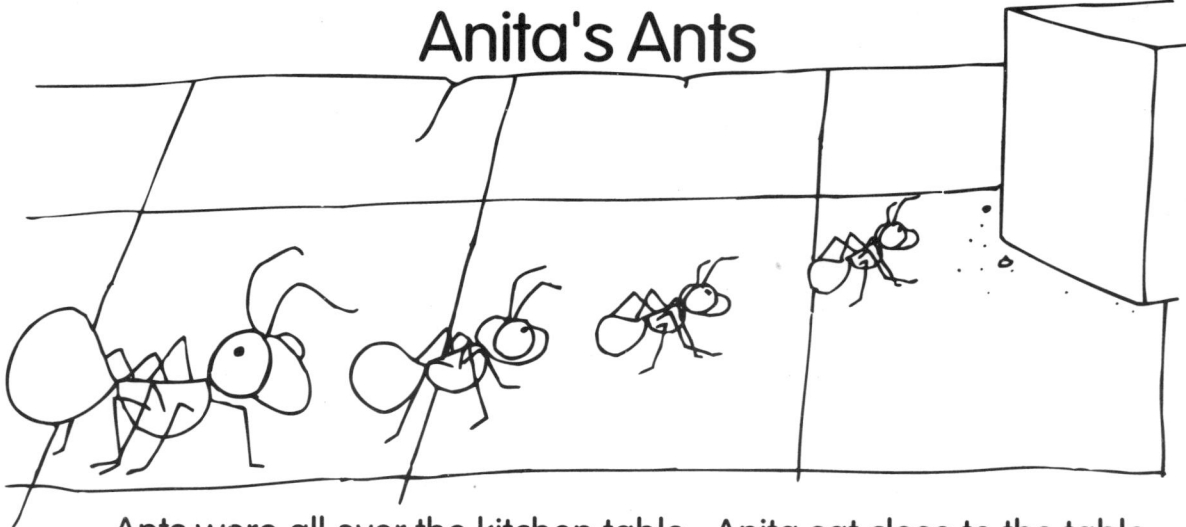

Ants were all over the kitchen table. Anita sat close to the table and watched the small insects. She didn't move even when one of the ants suddenly crawled onto her hand. It felt funny as it moved across her fingers.

Anita wondered if the ant was hungry. She picked up a crumb of bread and put it on her finger near the ant. The ant picked up the crumb and carried it away. Then Anita had an idea. She would make a safe place for the ants to find food.

She found a small box and put crumbs of bread, biscuits, and cheese in it. She put the box near the ants on the table. Soon the ants were crawling in and out of the box carrying the crumbs away. Anita felt happy for the ants.

When Anita's mother came home, she was surprised. "Ants are dirty, and we don't want them in the house," she said. She told Anita to carry the box outside and leave it there.

Anita missed watching the ants work.

Teacher: The main character.

Answer these questions about the **characters** in *Anita's Ants.*

1. List the people and animals in the story:

   _____   _____   _____

2. Who watched the ants?

   _____

3. Who made a box for the ants?

   _____

4. Who didn't want the ants in the house?

   _____

5. Who missed watching the ants when they were put outside?

   _____

6. Who do you think was the **main character** in this story?

   _____

   Tell why you picked this character.

   _____

   _____

   _____

   _____

   _____

Read and Think

Read this story.
Think about what happens.
Then number the steps in order on page 19.

Oatmeal Biscuits

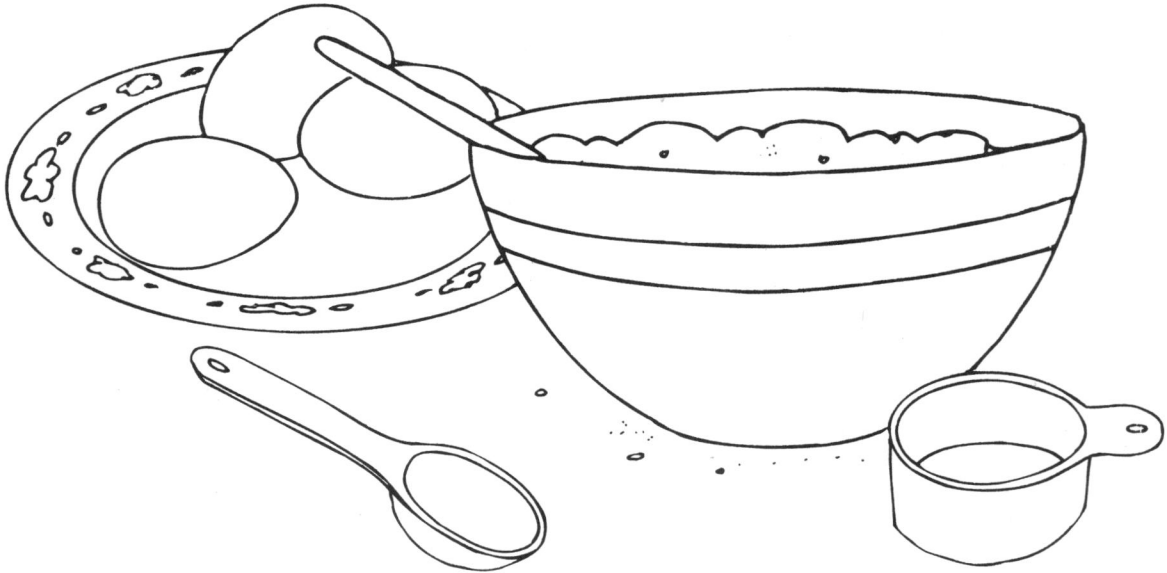

Michael loved oatmeal biscuits. He looked in the biscuit jar, but all the biscuits were gone. Michael decided to make biscuits himself.

He found the oatmeal box and put it on the table. He got eggs and milk from the refrigerator then Michael found the big mixing bowl. He broke two eggs into the bowl and poured in some milk. He was ready to put in the oatmeal when Dad came home.

"Wait a minute, son," Dad said. "We have to follow the recipe to make good biscuits. I will help you read the recipe, and you can mix the dough."

After they mixed the dough, Michael and his dad baked the biscuits in the oven. The work made them so hungry, they ate three biscuits before dinner.

Think about what happens in the story **Oatmeal Biscuits.**

Number the steps in the order they happened in the story.

_____ Michael got oatmeal, eggs, and milk.

___1___ All of the biscuits were gone.

_____ Dad came home and found Michael making biscuits.

_____ They each ate three biscuits before dinner.

_____ Michael decided to make biscuits.

_____ He broke the eggs and poured the milk into a big bowl.

_____ Dad stopped Michael. "Wait a minute, son."

_____ They baked the oatmeal biscuits.

_____ Dad Helped Michael read and follow the recipe.

More Sequencing

Sometimes a story does not tell what happened in the same order that the events really took place. Someone in the story might be thinking about something that happened at a different time. In this way, **time order** can be different than **story order**.

Read this little story.

At lunchtime, Monica was surprised to find a cupcake in her lunch box. Then she remembered that her father had made cupcakes the night before.

Number the **story order.**

_____ Monica was surprised to find a cupcake in her lunch box.

_____ Monica remembered her father making cupcakes the night before.

Here is the **time order** in which the story happened.
Do you see the difference?

1. Monica's father made cupcakes.

2. Monica was surprised to find a cupcake in her lunch box.

3. Monica remembered her father making cupcakes the night before.

Adam's House

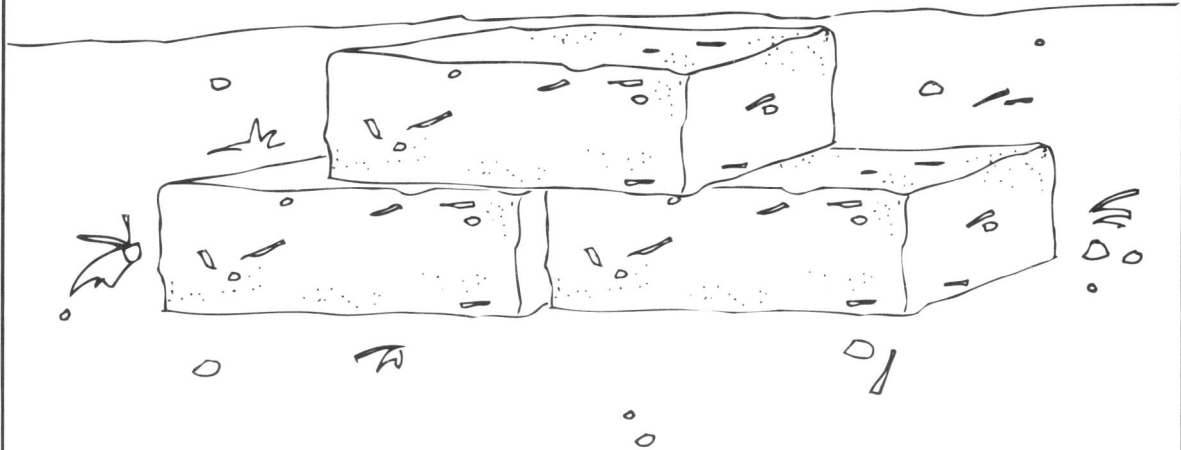

Adam wanted to build a house. He could not use wood because he did not have enough. He did have plenty of mud and straw, so he decided to make bricks. He mixed the mud with straw and grass so it would stick together. He used boxes to shape the mud into bricks. He left the bricks in the sun for a long time. When the bricks were dry and hard, Adam was able to build his house.

1. How did Adam make the mud stick together?

_____

2. How did Adam shape the bricks?

_____

3. How did Adam dry the bricks?

_____

Understanding **why** things happen is important.

John fixed his bike so he could go to the park.
   Why did John fix his bike?
   He fixed his bike so he could go to the park.

Read this story. Then answer the questions on page 23.

Carol and Ann

Carol was sad. Her best friend, Ann, had moved away. Carol would miss Ann for many reasons. The girls used to play together everyday. They liked to play with all of Ann's video games. Carol had a tennis racquet, and Ann had a bat and ball. They played rounders together. They both liked to go to the beach. They would swim and build sand castles.

Most of all Carol would miss having Ann to talk to everyday. They talked about their friends and families. They laughed at the funny things that happened. They helped each other when they had problems. Carol knew she would miss Ann a lot.

Answer these **why** questions about *Carol and Ann*.

1. Why was Carol sad?

_____

_____

2. Why did the girls go to the beach?

_____

_____

3. Why where the girls able to play rounders?

_____

_____

4. Why would Carol miss Ann?
   (Give at least two important reasons.)

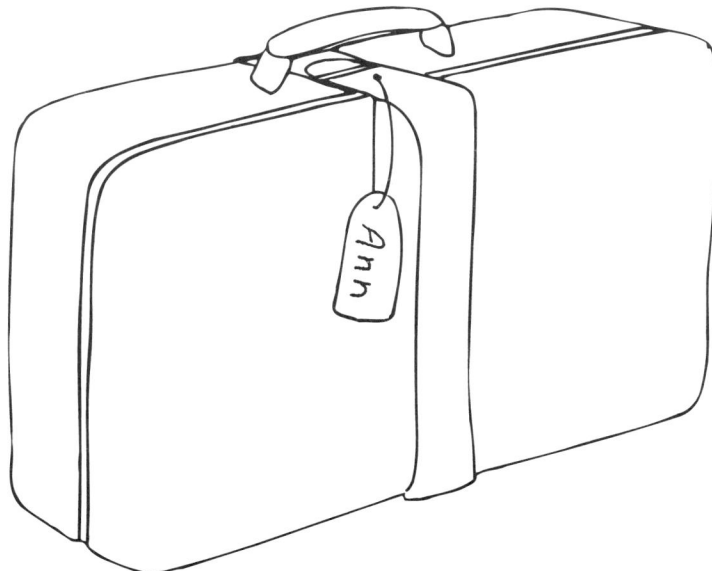

_____

_____

_____

_____

Use this story to practice the hints for previewing a story.
1. Read the title and the underlined headings in this story.
2. Go to page 25 and answer the questions in part 1.

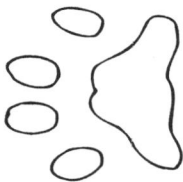

The Jaguar

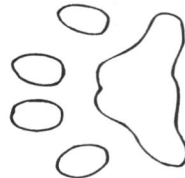

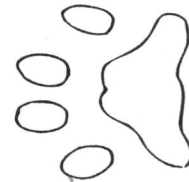

The jaguar is one of the many members of the cat family.

What It Looks Like

The jaguar is a member of the cat family. It is smaller, but heavier than a mountain lion. Its coat is deep yellow or brownish-yellow. It is marked with many dark spots.

Where It Lives

The jaguar lives in the rainforests of Central and South America. It likes to lie on tree branches to rest and watch for prey.

What It Eats

The jaguar's favourite foods are animals such as peccaries, capybaras, mountain sheep, and ground-living birds.

After the lion and the tiger, the jaguar is the strongest cat on Earth.

Answer these questions about *The Jaguar.*

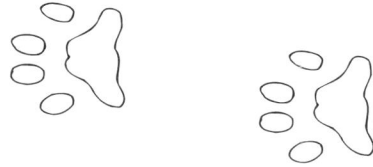

Part 1
The **headings** on page 24 told me I will find out these three things about a jaguar.

1. _____

2. _____

3. _____

Now, go back to page 24.
Read the **first sentence** and the **last sentence** of the story.
When you have finished, do part 2.

Part 2
Answer these questions in your own words.

1. What did the first sentence of the story tell you?

_____

2. What did the last sentence of the story tell you?

_____

Now, go back to page 24 and read the **whole story.** When you have finished, come back and answer the questions in part 3.

Part 3
1. What are the markings on a jaguar?

_____

2. Where does the jaguar live?

_____

3. What are two of the jaguar's favourite foods?

_____

Monkeys

The bodies of monkeys are perfect for living in trees. They have long, slender bodies and handy tails. They can use their tails to help them climb. They can grab things with both their hands and their feet.

Monkeys eat many things. They like leaves, buds, fruits, and insects. Sometimes they eat bird eggs. Monkeys usually eat in the morning and afternoon, but will also snack at other times of the day.

Most monkeys like to live in groups. These groups may have as many as 100 monkeys. Monkeys enjoy caring for their babies and playing together. They chatter a lot and seem to understand each other's noises.

Monkeys do not make good pets. They are very noisy and lively. Sometimes they destroy things by accident. They are curious animals and use their hands to try to get inside things.

Monkeys are clever and playful. They are good at putting things together and taking them apart. They like to play in trees or on the bars of their cages at the zoo. Most people enjoy watching monkeys swing and jump from place to place.

What I Learned in **Monkeys:**

1. What did the title tell you this story is about?

_____

_____

2. What did you learn about the monkey's body?

_____

_____

3. What do monkeys eat?

_____

_____

4. What did you learn about why monkeys live in groups?

_____

_____

5. Why don't monkeys make good pets?

_____

_____

6. In what ways are monkeys clever and playful.

_____

_____

> **Details** are the parts of a story that give us more information.
> about the **main idea**.

Read this story, then answer the questions at the bottom of the page.

The Moon

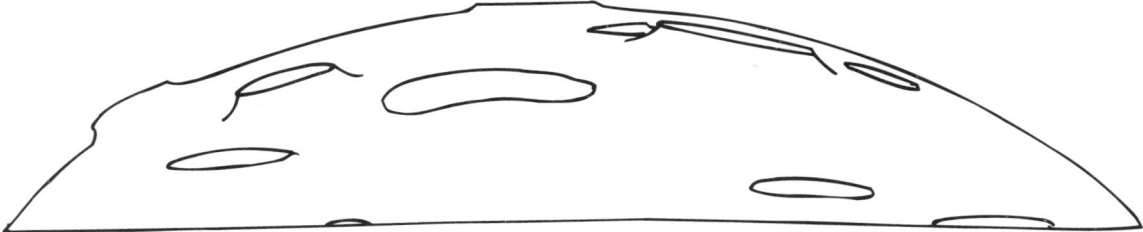

Our moon is very different from the planet we live on. It is smaller in size than the Earth. The surface is rocky, barren, greyish, and covered with a layer of fine dust. There are high mountains, flat areas, and craters. Because there is no air on the moon, sound cannot travel. Because there is no wind, footprints in the dust stay there forever.

_____

1. Write the most important idea in this story (**main idea**).

_____

_____

_____

2. Write the other information you learned about the moon (**details**).

_____

_____

_____

_____

_____

As you begin to read a paragraph, it's fun to **predict** what will happen in the rest of a paragraph.

Read this part of a paragraph.
Try to **predict** what will happen in the rest of this paragraph.

Karen

Karen wanted to have a party. She thought about what it might be like. She liked to play catch with her new ball. She liked to swim and play in the sand at the beach. She wanted to see lots of her friends all playing together.

What do you think might happen next?
Write your **prediction** here.

_____

_____

_____

_____

Turn this page upside down and read what happened next.
See if your prediction was the same as this ending.

Karen asked her mother if she could have a beach party. Her mother said, "Yes, I will help you plan it." Karen and her mother invited all of Karen's friends. The friends played catch with Karen's new ball. Then they swam in the sea and built sand castles on the beach.

29

Teacher: Explain prediction to children.

Goldilocks and the Three Bears

1. Cut sentences apart.
2. Put in correct order.
3. Paste to answer sheet.
4. Read your story to a friend.

The bears came home and found Goldilocks.

She sat on baby bear's chair and broke it.

Goldilocks ran away and never came back again.

Goldilocks opened the door and went into bears' house.

She went upstairs and fell asleep in baby bear's bed.

Goldilocks tasted the porridge. She ate baby bear's all up.

One day the three bears went for a walk in the woods while their porridge cooled.

Now try this.   1. Colour the bears brown.
2. Make Goldilocks' hair yellow.
3. Draw Baby Bear's chair.

Teacher: Simple sequencing.

Goldilocks and
the Three Bears

1.

2.

3.

4.

5.

6.

7.

31

Teacher: Paste sentences in correct order.

Little Red Riding Hood

1. Cut sentences apart.
2. Put in correct order.
3. Paste to answer sheet.
4. Read your story to a friend.

Little Red Riding Hood was on her way to Grandma's house. Grandma was sick, so Red Riding Hood was taking her some good things to eat.

The wolf took a short cut to Grandma's house. He made her think he was Red Riding Hood. He gobbled poor Grandma up. He put on her cap and got into her bed.

"Grandma, what big teeth you have," said Red Riding Hood. "The better to eat you with," said the wolf. He began to chase her around the room.

The woodcutter cut the wolf open and out came Grandma. He took the wolf skin away. Then they ate all the good things from Red Riding Hood's basket.

She met a wolf in the woods. "Hello, little girl," said the wolf. "Where are you going?" "I am going to my Grandma's house with a basket of good things to eat," said Red Riding Hood.

When Red Riding Hood got to Grandma's house, she went in and said, "Grandma, what big eyes you have." "The better to see you with." "What big ears you have." "The better to hear you with."

A woodcutter heard Red Riding Hood shout for help. He came with his axe and killed the wolf.

Now try this.
1. Colour her cape red.
2. Make the wolf brown.
3. Draw stripes on Grandma's quilt.

Little Red Riding Hood

1.

2.

3.

4.

5.

6.

7.

The Gingerbread Boy

1. Cut sentences apart.
2. Put in correct order.
3. Paste to answer sheet.
4. Read your story to a friend.

The gingerbread boy ran on and on. He ran away from the horse and the cow. He ran away from the mower and the thresher. No one could catch him.

The gingerbread boy jumped out of the oven. He ran out the door and down the road.

A fox was by the river, he said "I will take you across the river. Jump up on my back." The gingerbread boy did.

Once upon a time there was an old lady. One day she made a gingerbread boy for her husband. She put it into the oven to bake.

The gingerbread boy came to a river. He had to go across the water to get away.

The old woman and the old man ran after the gingerbread boy. They did not catch him.

The fox went into deep water. The gingerbread boy jumped up on the fox's head. The fox ate the gingerbread boy all up.

Now try this.
1. Colour the fox red.
2. Make the gingerbread boy brown.
3. Draw ripples in the river.

The Gingerbread Boy

1.

2.

3.

4.

5.

6.

7.

The Little Red Hen

1. Cut sentences apart.
2. Put in correct order.
3. Paste to answer sheet.
4. Read your story to a friend.

"Who will plant this seed?" she asked. "We won't," said the Cat, the Dog and the Rat. "Then I will," said the Little Red Hen.

Little Red Hen found a wheat seed one day.

"The wheat was made into flour at the mill. "Who will make the flour into bread?" she asked. "We won't," said the Cat, the Dog and the Rat. "Then I will," said the Little Red Hen.

The wheat grew tall and yellow. "Who will cut the wheat?" she asked. "We won't," said the Cat, the Dog and the Rat. "Then I will," said the Little Red Hen.

"Who will eat this bread?" she asked. "We will!" said the Cat, the Dog and the Rat. "Oh, no you won't!" said the Little Red Hen.

"Who will take the wheat to the mill?" she asked. "We won't," said the Cat, the Dog and the Rat. "Then I will," said the Little Red Hen.

Little Red Hen called her chicks. They ate up all the bread.

Now try this.   1.   Colour the hen red and orange.
2.   Make the dog brown with black spots.
3.   Draw four little chicks.

The Little Red Hen

1.

2.

3.

4.

5.

6.

7.

The Three Billy Goats Gruff

1. Cut sentences apart.
2. Put in correct order.
3. Paste to answer sheet.
4. Read your story to a friend.

Big Billy Goat Gruff hit the troll so hard that he was never seen again.

Once upon a time there were three goats named Gruff. They wanted to go across a bridge to eat grass on the hillside.

The second billy Goat Gruff went across the bridge. "I'm going to eat you up!" said the troll. "I'm too little. Wait for my brother. He is bigger," said the second goat. So the troll did.

At last the big Billy Goat Gruff came to the bridge. "I'm going to eat you up!" said the troll. "Come up and try," said Big Billy Goat Gruff. So the troll did.

Now the three goats go over the bridge to the hillside to eat grass every day.

Under the bridge lived a bad troll with big eyes and a long nose. He liked to eat goats.

One day the little Billy Goat Gruff went across the bridge. "I'm going to eat you up!" said the troll. "I'm too little. Wait for my brother. He is bigger," said the little goat. So the troll did.

Now try this.   1.   Give the troll red hair.
2.   Make the sky blue.
3.   Draw water under the bridge.

The Three
Billy Goats
Gruff

1.

2.

3.

4.

5.

6.

7.

The Three Little Pigs

1. Cut sentences apart.
2. Put in correct order.
3. Paste to answer sheet.
4. Read your story to a friend.

One day three little pigs went out to find new homes. The first pig built his house of straw. Along came a wolf. He blew the straw house down and ate the pig.

The third little pig built his house of bricks. Along came the wolf. He huffed and puffed, but he could not blow down the brick house.

The wolf was angry. "I will come down the chimney," he said. The little pig put a pot of hot water on the fire. The wolf fell into the hot water. The little pig was safe at last.

He tried to trick the third little pig. "Come to the turnip patch. We can get good turnips to eat." The little pig was smart. He went before the wolf got to the patch.

The second pig built his house out of sticks. Along came the wolf. He blew the stick house down and ate the little pig.

Next the wolf tried to trick the pig into going for apples with him. The pig was smart. He went before the wolf got to the apple tree.

The wolf tried one more time. "Meet me at the fair." he said. This time the wolf went early too. The pig hid in a butter churn and rolled home so the wolf did not see him.

Now try this.
1. Colour the pig pink.
2. Make the wolf grey.
3. Draw flowers in the pig's flowerbox.

The Three Little Pigs

1.

2.

3.

4.

5.

6.

7.

Jack and the Beanstalk

1. Cut sentences apart.
2. Put in correct order.
3. Paste to answer sheet.
4. Read your story to a friend.

The next morning, Jack saw a large beanstalk growing up to the sky. He went up the beanstalk. When Jack reached the top, he saw a large castle and went in.

On his second trip up the beanstalk, Jack took a sack of gold from the sleeping giant.

Once there was a poor woman and her son Jack. All they had left was a cow. One day Mother sent Jack to town to sell the cow. He met a man on the road to town. Jack traded the cow for a magic bean.

Soon a giant came into the castle. Jack hid. He saw the giant with a hen that laid golden eggs. When the giant fell asleep, Jack took the hen and ran home with it.

Jack went up the beanstalk one more time. This time he took a singing harp from the sleeping giant and ran from the castle. The singing harp woke up the giant. He chased Jack down the beanstalk.

When Jack returned home, Mother asked, "What did you get for the cow?" Jack gave the magic bean to his mother. She became upset and threw the bean out the window. Jack was sent to bed with no supper.

When Jack got down to the bottom of the beanstalk, he grabbed an axe and chopped down the beanstalk. The giant fell to the ground and was never seen again.

Now try this. 1. Colour the giant's hair red.
2. Draw the golden egg.
3. Draw a green beanstalk to help Jack get away.

Jack and the Beanstalk

1.

2.

3.

4.

5.

6.

7.

The Emperor's New Clothes

1. Cut sentences apart.
2. Put in correct order.
3. Paste to answer sheet.
4. Read your story to a friend.

After a while, the Emperor sent someone to see the cloth. The two men were pretending to make the magic cloth. The Emperor's man did not see anything, but he didn't want anyone to call him a fool, so he said, "How pretty it is."

The Emperor decided to see the cloth for himself. He didn't see anything. "Am I a fool? That cannot be. No one must know." So the Emperor said, "How pretty it is."

The men pretended to make a suit from the magic cloth. The Emperor still could not see the cloth, but he let the men dress him in the suit.

Long ago there lived an Emperor who loved clothes. He had no time for anything else. One day, two men came and said to the Emperor, "We can weave magic cloth."

Everyone was waiting to see the new suit of magic cloth. As the Emperor marched down the street, no one could see the cloth, but they all said, "How pretty it is."

The Emperor wanted a suit of magic cloth. "Then I can tell who the fools are in my kingdom," he said. He paid the two men a lot of money to make the magic cloth.

Suddenly a child said, "The Emperor has nothing on." The Emperor knew it was true.

Now try this.
1. Colour the emperor's underwear yellow.
2. Make his cape purple.
3. Draw a crown for the Emperor.

The Emperor's New Clothes

1.

2.

3.

4.

5.

6.

7.

Rumplestiltskin

1. Cut sentences apart.
2. Put in correct order.
3. Paste to answer sheet.
4. Read your story to a friend.

When the king left, she began to cry. She didn't know how to spin straw into gold. The door opened and a funny-looking little man came in. "Give me your necklace and I will spin the straw into gold," he said. By morning the straw was gold.

The third time the king left the girl to spin, she had nothing to give the funny-looking little man. "Then promise to give me your first child." The girl did promise and he spun the straw into gold.

A poor farmer told the king that his daughter could spin straw into gold. The king wanted to see this, so he put the girl in a room at the castle, filled it with straw and a spinning wheel and left her to spin the straw into gold.

The king married the girl and made her Queen. A year later she had a baby. She had forgotten her promise. The funny-looking little man came for her baby.

The king put her into another room of straw. This time the girl gave the funny-looking man her ring. Again he spun all the straw into gold.

The first two days she guessed wrong. On the third day a messenger returned and said, "I heard a little man singing in the woods." He told the queen the name. When the little man came, she said, "Your name is Rumplestiltskin ." He was very angry.

When the queen begged him not to take the baby, he said, "I will not take the baby if you can guess my name in the next three days."

Now try this.   1. Colour the Queen's gown orange and blue.
2. Make Rumplestiltskin green.
3. Draw the yellow straw.

Rumplestiltskin

1.

2.

3.

4.

5.

6.

7.

One way to enjoy reading is to think of your own ending to the story. Read this story starter. Then choose the ending you like best.

The Perfect Holiday

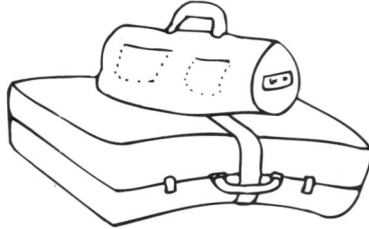

Louis **was excited.** He knew that this holiday would be fun. His father promised to take Louis and his sister Anna to a very special place. They had planned the trip for a long time. Tomorrow they would leave. Louis could hardly wait!

Mark the ending you like best.

☐ In the morning, Louis and Anna and their father packed the car. They packed all their camping gear in the trunk. They packed their clothes in bags. Then they drove to the mountains.

They made a camp and then went for a swim in the river. The next day they rode horses to the biggest waterfall. They rode a raft through the rapids in the river and hiked through the mountains. It was a perfect holiday.

_____

☐ In the morning, Louis and Anna and their father flew in an aeroplane to Paris. They checked into the hotel. They had dinner at a restaurant in the hotel.

The next day they went to Euro Disney. They rode on many rides and played video games. They explored the many exhibits and ate all kinds of food. It was a perfect holiday.

Teacher: Read both endings aloud to children.